Civil Rights Challenges of the 21st Century: A View from the States

United States Commission on Civil Rights

Staff Report
Publication Date

Table of Contents

Purpose

The Commission on Civil Rights' unique statutory mandate affords it the enviable opportunity to continue to enhance enforcement of civil rights laws and to appraise laws and policies of the Federal government with respect to the civil rights challenges of the 21st Century. The Commission is uniquely poised to answer these questions: What civil rights issues and remedies will emerge over the next five, 10 and 25 years? What are the thorniest challenges facing enforcement agencies and the private bar in safeguarding fundamental civil rights in an era of dwindling resources? What are the most promising enforcement strategies for identifying pervasive discrimination and for promoting equal opportunity for all? What are the root causes of disparities in health, education, housing and wealth, and are disparities caused by discrimination?

As our new Strategic Plan mandates, the Commission hopes to answer these questions and shape a national conversation on current civil rights issues by publishing this report, which presents the top civil rights issues across our many states as identified by State Advisory Committee (SAC) members. This report utilizes the advisory committees to identify for policy-makers, researchers, and the public state and regional civil rights issues and priorities. This staff report contains a state-by-state ranking of the top civil rights issues as identified by SAC members, background information on the composition of the various SACs, and some discussion of the top-ranked issues in the respective civil rights fields, e.g., race/color, sex, age, disability.

This report will hopefully enable the Commission to obtain an on-the-ground perspective in regions and states in identifying top civil rights priorities. This perspective in turn will help the Commission meet its Strategic Goal of shaping a national conversation on current and future civil rights issues that identifies civil rights priorities for policy makers.

The SACs: Composition and Function

The Commission is required by statute to establish and maintain 51 independent SACs—one for each state and the District of Columbia. These SACs are chartered under the Federal Advisory Committee Act. The members serve without compensation as special government employees and assist the Commission with its fact-finding, investigative, and information dissemination functions. Their term of office is two years, but they can be reappointed. These SACs function as the Commission's "eyes and ears" throughout the Nation. Under their respective charters and the Commission's regulation at 45 C.F.R. § 703.2, the SACs:

> a) Advise the Commission in writing of any knowledge or information it has of any alleged deprivation of the right to vote and to have the vote counted by reason of color, race, religion, sex, age, disability, or national origin, or that citizens are being accorded or denied the right to vote in Federal elections as a result of patterns or practices of fraud or discrimination;

> (b) Advise the Commission concerning matters related to discrimination or a denial of equal protection of the laws under the Constitution and the effect of the laws and policies of the Federal Government with respect to equal protection of the laws;

(c) Advise the Commission upon matters of mutual concern in the preparation of reports of the Commission to the President and the Congress;

(d) Receive reports, suggestions, and recommendations from individuals, public and private organizations, and public officials upon matters pertinent to inquiries conducted by the Advisory Committee;

(e) Initiate and forward advice and recommendations to the Commission upon matters that the Advisory Committee has studied;

(f) Assist the Commission in the exercise of its clearinghouse function and with respect to other matters that the Advisory Committee has studied;

(g) Attend, as observers, any open hearing or conference that the Commission may hold within the State.

Pursuant to the Commission's Administrative Instruction (AI) 5-9, *Procedures for Recommending State Advisory Committee Appointments,* the members of the Commission are responsible for appointing all SAC members and for designating one member to serve asChair.

The Commission's regulation at 45 C.F.R.§ 703.5(b), provides that "no person is to be denied an opportunity to serve on a State Advisory Committee because of race, age, sex, religion, national origin, or disability." It also provides that the Commission "shall encourage membership on the State Advisory Committees to be broadly diverse." AI 5-9 provides further guidance to ensure that SAC nominations are not biased toward or against a particular viewpoint, gender, race, religion, age, national origin, or disability status. AI 5-9 § 2.02 provides that "membership shall not be established to ensure or limit a certain percentage for representation of any racial or ethnic group." AI 5-9 § 2.04 echoes the requirement under the Federal Advisory Committee Act that membership shall "be fairly balanced in terms of the points of view represented and the functions to be performed." AI 5-9 § 7.09 provides that "both political parties should be represented in each State Advisory Committee," without setting a quota or cap on political affiliation. AI 5-9 further recommends that members represent a diversity of skills and experiences, including but not limited to social science research, legal research and analysis, and statistical analysis; that representation from educators, lawyers, business and labor leaders, social scientists, researchers and news gatherers be encouraged; that SACs should contain people knowledgeable of the state's governmental machinery and public service sector and people drawn from sectors such as business and financial communities, organized labor, the news media, and religious groups; and that each SAC should contain people with a demonstrated interest in civil rights issues, including those pertaining to color, race, religion, sex, age, disability, and national origin, and voting rights.

Methodology

In order to obtain SAC member input on the top issues facing their respective states, the Commission requested that SAC members identify the top civil rights issues and challenges facing their states among the civil rights areas that fall within our statutory mandate:

- o Race/Color/National Origin
- o Gender
- o Religion
- o Age
- o Disability
- o Voting rights
- o Administration of Justice

We requested this input in three stages. These three stages were intended to provide us with clear and transparent results, avoid ambiguities and duplications among the suggestions made, and promote specificity among the same.

First, we invited all SAC members to submit a list of his or her state's top civil rights issues among the categories listed above. At this stage, members were asked to identify all issues that they consider to be important, without any limitation as to number. Based on this first set of responses, staff distilled the results of this initial inquiry into a "master" list that contained the submissions of all SAC members who responded, regardless of state. This comprehensive list of all suggestions made provided each SAC the benefits of ideas suggested by members of other SACs. This comprehensive list also allowed staff to group similar suggestions into common categories.

Second, we distributed the master list to all SAC members. This gave members a second opportunity to identify additional issues in case they believed that there were significant omissions in the collective response.

In the third and final inquiry, we asked each SAC member to rank his or her state's top five civil rights issues in order of preference in each of the categories described above, with "1" being the highest, "2" the second highest, etc. The Office of the Staff Director (OSD) then tabulated the results for each state, identifying the top issues in each category according to the SAC members' rankings.

The Issues

SAC members elaborated their concerns more specifically with respect to these civil rights issues:

Race/Color/National Origin

- *Enforcement of/compliance with state civil rights initiatives that prohibit discrimination or preferential treatment on the basis race in education, employment, or public contracting.* A California SAC member referred to a study conducted on the University of Michigan admissions policies showing possible violations of its state initiative. She also noted that the Michigan Department of Transportation was seeking approval of a race conscious goal in its federally funded public contracts.

- *The racial/ethnic achievement gap in elementary and secondary education in public schools and its possible causes (e.g., family structure, culture, underfunded schools).* A member of the California SAC called the ongoing failure of the state's public schools in major urban areas to meet basic educational needs for inner city minority students a local and national disgrace. Moreover, he called compulsory school attendance laws unjustifiably coercive because parents are not empowered to select a better school for their child. This restriction is particularly onerous where school conditions involve prevalent drug use and threats of violence and intimidation. He believed the state's statistics in terms of racial/ethnic gaps in attrition, graduation, and levels of academic achievement merit urgent attention. A member of the Texas SAC pointed to the growing achievement gap between Hispanic and non-Hispanic students and believed it imperative to assess what has and has not worked to close this gap, including the No Child Left Behind Act. A Wisconsin SAC member stated that hypotheses other than discrimination are equally plausible in explaining these gaps, including that the culture of the community does not emphasize learning, that single-parents are unable to provide an environment conducive to learning, and that schools are underfunded, among others. He argues that if the strength of these other hypotheses was identified, then it would be possible to focus in a more targeted way on the role of discrimination (whatever it might be) in affecting minority student achievement.

- *Racial and ethnic preferences in admissions in colleges and universities and their impact on intended beneficiaries.* One California SAC member related that two of the campuses in her state university system changed their undergraduate admissions policies from comprehensive review to holistic review of student applications. According to her, information from a professor at one of these campuses indicates that the change was specially designed to admit more underrepresented minorities and that the process has led to using race as a factor in reviewing the applications. She expressed her frustration at the secrecy surrounding the process and the lack of disclosure on the part of universities about their admissions practices. A member of the Wisconsin SAC stated his belief that these preferences are based on a deep-seated belief that minority groups should be treated differently and preferentially because of slavery, discrimination, family background, etc. He cited his own studies and writing that attempt to demonstrate that preferential treatment is given on the basis of race, color, and national origin, that doing so is wrong, that this practice has adverse effects on the very groups it is attempting to help, that this practice helps to stereotype minorities as being less capable than they are, and that the goal of trying to increase minority enrollments through the use of preferences (i.e., admitting minorities who are not academically competitive with non-minority students) undermines the goal of increasing minority student graduation rates.

- *The use of employment discrimination law concepts such as hostile environment as a justification for restrictions on freedom of expression in higher education.* A Wisconsin SAC member stated that this tendency has been most apparent in the development of college and university policies on sexual and other forms of harassment. According to him, these policies, in attempting to create a more friendly and welcoming environment for minorities and females, draw upon the concept of a hostile work environment as justification for policies and procedures that restrict freedom of expression and run counter to the very idea of a university, which is to promote truth regardless of what awkward issues might come up in the process of that search. He argues that a document dealing with these distinctions would be helpful to everyone in higher education.

- *Employment of women and racial/ethnic minorities in state agencies.* A member of the Kentucky SAC referred us to the state's biannual report of women and minorities in state agencies, which reported that minorities comprised 9.28 percent of the state workforce (8 percent African-American, 0.42 percent "other," 0.37 percent Asian-American, 0.35 percent Hispanics, and 0.16 American Indians).

- *Possible racial disparate impact of employer's use of credit reports in hiring decisions.* One SAC member related her personal experience in not being hired for a position due to an unacceptable credit report rating, despite being qualified for the job. She expressed her concern that such a practice affected more people of color and minorities than whites because of their economic status in urban centers. She further expressed concern about this practice as it applies to non-bank jobs and the regulatory framework governing such a practice.

- *Racial disparities in health care, education, housing, wealth, and incarceration, and their relationship to each other and to possible causes, such as family structure and inherited intelligence potential that differs by individual.* One member of the Illinois SAC related a recent report by the Applied Research Center that found that the median net worth of white households was six times that of households of color. She attributed racial gaps in housing, health care, education, and employment to this income disparity. A member of the Michigan SAC placed the blame for the disparities in housing, health care, wealth, and incarceration with educational disparities. He traces the educational disparities primarily to differences in attitudes towards education and in preparedness for education, which themselves stem from differences in both nurture (such as peer pressure and stability of family structure) and nature (inherited intelligence potential known to differ by individuals and not known to differ by group).

- *Discrimination against Hispanic individuals in employment, education, or housing based on race or presumed immigration status.* A member of the Utah SAC believes that we have increasingly built our economy around undocumented workers yet there continues to be a public outcry against their presence. According to this SAC member, this situation leads to a racist and discriminatory attitude toward both legal and illegal immigrants.

- *The lack of comprehensive immigration law combining border security with respect for the dignity of the human person and its contribution to the alienation of immigrants from participating in mainstream society.* A member of the Texas SAC pointed to the rising number of illegal immigrants and the lack of comprehensive immigration reform. He expressed his concern that, until a feasible guest worker program was implemented, many illegal immigrants would continue to live in the shadows and not be full participants in American democracy. He believed that recent immigration raids only served to further alienate illegal immigrants from mainstream society. Finally, he stated that a solution that effectively combines border security and simultaneously respects the dignity of the person and his right to make a living for his family must be addressed in the next several years.

- *Discrimination against Native Americans.* A member of the California SAC stated that it was not clear how state governments are to treat Native Americans (compare *Morton v. Mancari* with *Adarand Constructors v. Pena*). She asked whether Native Americans were a racial classification or a political classification under these cases. She also asked whether tribes were entitled to sovereign immunity when a negligent act occurred outside of a reservation. According to her, these questions bear examination because they impact business in California where tribal gambling profits are being used to buy businesses that provide services off the reservation.

- *Possible extension of tribal recognition and quasi-sovereignty to Native Hawaiians.* One member of the Hawaii SAC described passage of the Akaka bill as "the worst blunder the seniors of our country and society can make." Another member of the Hawaii SAC argued that this legislation would create a privileged class consisting of anyone with at least one ancestor indigenous to the lands now part of the United States and sponsor the creation of a separate sovereign government in Hawaii of, by and for persons with an ancestor indigenous to Hawaii. He also notes that the bill did not require that new government to be subject to the full reach of the Constitution or the civil rights laws of the United States or the State of Hawaii and that it authorizes negotiations for the breakup and giveaway to that new government of some unspecified amount of Hawaii's land, natural resources, governmental power and civil and criminal jurisdiction.

- *Discrimination against non-native Hawaiians in the provision of governmental services / The Office of Hawaiian Affairs' acceptance of certain state lands and cash in settlement of Native Hawaiian claims to reparations for the transfer of certain lands from the Hawaiian monarchy to the Republic of Hawaii and subsequently to the State of Hawaii.* One SAC member noted that this discrimination could impact how Native Americans are treated in her own state.

- *Disparate impact/treatment of racially identifiable populations in the contexts of law enforcement (racial profiling), sentencing, and incarceration (e.g., prison conditions, use of rehabilitative ex-offender programs).* One member of the Ohio SAC expressed his view that incarceration was the end of a causal chain. He suggested that the problem can be unsatisfactorily but very directly ameliorated by releasing minority prisoners, but that this may result in a detrimental influence on the communities into which they would be released. Rather, he said, the problem can be satisfactorily solved by addressing issues that occur far earlier in the causal chain, rather than focusing solely on law enforcement policies and procedures. A member of the Illinois SAC recommended treatment programs to provide counseling and other rehabilitative services to these individuals, as well as effective ex-offender programs to create job opportunities and thus productive citizens. Another member of the Illinois SAC recommended that we examine the possibility of disparate treatment in sentencing of racial minorities, who continue to be disproportionately represented in the incarcerated population. She also recommended that racial profiling and mistreatment by police be carefully monitored.

- *The impact of minority neighborhoods plagued by crime, drugs and violence on access to education, and possible solutions to this problem (e.g., job training, assiduous policing, family structure).* A member of the Ohio SAC recounted hearing a minority group member speak on the radio about the plight of his elderly parents, who are afraid to leave their house because their neighborhood is plagued by crime, drugs, and violence. He also recounted the case of a public official walking a child to school in Columbus on "Walk a Child to School Day," only to be told by the child to take an indirect route because the direct route was down a street often plagued by gunfire. This SAC member argued that the school would be more effective if its students were not threatened with death on the way to school. He believed the problem may be largely attributable to the incidence of fatherless boys and thus would require a cultural shift in the communities themselves.

- *The provision of equal educational opportunities to disadvantaged students of color.* One South Carolina SAC member traced unequal educational opportunities to the property tax structure of school funding in many states. According to this member, many students of color, especially those residing in rural or inner cities, are not being afforded the same level or quality of educational resources and opportunities as those provided to their suburban, white counterparts. She urged the Commission to study these inequities and make recommendations to the federal and state governments to amend these inherently unequal funding structures. An Illinois SAC member described her state's public schools as chronically underfunded, and she traces the schools' crumbling infrastructure, lack of basic supplies, security concerns, and severe overcrowding to this lack of resources. Finally, she expressed her particular concern that this situation has a disparate negative impact on African-American and Hispanic students whose families cannot afford private schools or relocate to another district.

- *Enforcement of minority business enterprises (MBE) and women business enterprises (WBE) guidance in state and federal contracting, including race- and gender-based hiring goals, and the lack of opportunities for public contracting for these enterprises.* One

California SAC member argued that the more pressing issue was whether public agencies that receive federal funding can use race and sex preferences in awarding public contracts. She noted that the California Department of Transportation had set certain public contracting goals, a portion of which were to be achieved through race-conscious measures. She argued that federal regulations do not require race-conscious measures and public agencies should be required to exhaust race-neutral measures before resorting to race-conscious measures. A member of the Indiana SAC felt that, with respect to required participation levels of MBEs and WBEs in public contracting, a certain percentage must contribute to the direct line of business to encourage mainstream business to help build capacity with the field. A member of the Pennsylvania SAC stated that it is often difficult for minority and women-owned firms to access working capital and other loan assistance at competitive rates. She also stated that there still appears to be a lack of meaningful contracting opportunities actually afforded to these businesses.

- *Discrimination against undocumented immigrant workers in the areas of education and employment.* A member of the California SAC identified illegal immigration as a serious issue in the border states. She thought a comprehensive review of this issue as it relates to education and employment would be useful.

- *Race- and religion-motivated hate crimes.* An Illinois SAC member noted that more violent crimes based on religion, race and national origin seem to be occurring with a greater frequency. She noted a racially motivated shooting spree that killed Ricky Byrdsong in a suburb of Chicago, an increase in hate crimes committed against Muslims after 9/11, and the vandalization of a Jewish cemetery outside of Chicago by a neo-Nazi.

- *Racial discrimination in the context of national security.* A member of the Utah SAC stated that the continued tension in response to real and perceived national security threats would likely lead to discrimination against members of various ethnic groups and attempts to restrict civil liberties for everyone in dangerous ways.

- *Ensuring educational and extracurricular involvement of all students regardless of race, gender or national origin.* A member of the Kentucky SAC related an out-of-court settlement between a parent and school regarding a male student's desire to participate in cheerleading.

Gender

- *Lack of adequate legal protection for abused women and children.* An Illinois SAC member believes this issue to be problematic for women generally and because it disproportionately impacts low-income women and children who are racial minorities.

Disability

- *Discrimination (including employment) against people with mental health issues.* An Illinois SAC member understands that it is sometimes difficult for an employer to provide a reasonable accommodation to an employee suffering with severe depression or traumatic stress syndrome, but stressed that we must find ways to deal with this growing employment issue through tolerance, vocational rehabilitation, and education.

Religion

- ***Increase in religious discrimination in public education as a result of secularized curricula, religious expression by students, and religious immigrants.*** A member of the Connecticut SAC expressed his belief that secularized curricula may lead to claims that it constitutes discrimination against Christians. He also noted other potential for anti-religious discrimination against religious believers: how a school addresses gay marriage in teaching, whether students may display an outward sign of religious beliefs, and whether these issues will be heightened with the growing percentage of immigrants, who tend to be more religious-minded than other Americans.

- ***The impact on civil rights of religious employers, health care providers and other individuals as a result of governmental mandates that contravene widely-subscribed religious beliefs (e.g., coverage of contraceptives in employer health care plans; provision of controversial medical care; recognition of same-sex marriage).*** One Missouri SAC member stated his belief that such mandates were a direct violation of the Free Exercise guarantee of the First Amendment and related an attempt within his state's legislature to impose such a mandate. A member of the Connecticut SAC expressed his concern that legal battles on these issues may involve courts in deciding how "religious" a group must be and whether the challenged practice is seen as having a significant impact on the group's beliefs.

- ***The extent to which religious organizations can hire based on religion when they receive government funding.*** A member of the Connecticut SAC drew attention to the question of whether receipt of such funding authorizes the government to regulate hiring and other aspects of the organization.

- ***Conflict between assertion of some civil rights and the rights of free exercise, freedom of speech, and freedom of assembly, e.g., possible increase in religious discrimination as a result of laws prohibiting discrimination on the basis of sexual orientation.*** A member of the Illinois SAC mentioned that in California an obstetrician faced loss of his medical license for refusing -- based on his religious beliefs -- to perform a medical procedure that would allow a lesbian couple to conceive a child. He also mentioned an Illinois case in which a pharmacist faces loss of licensure for refusing -- based on religious conviction -- to supply an abortifacient. According to this SAC member, in both situations the complainants have numerous other doctors/pharmacists available to service their reproductive rights. He expressed his hope that mature leaders in civil rights could play an important role in leading public opinion into the understanding of how conflicting civil rights (right of reproduction and right of conscience) should be reconciled and coexist in a tolerant society.

- ***Increase in religious discrimination, including against religious minorities and non-religious citizenry.*** A Utah SAC member worried that the political culture seems to impose a litmus test of religious behavior for viable candidates for public office that may spill over into society.

Voting Rights

- ***Implementation and effectiveness of 'motor voter' legislation.*** One SAC member recommended an audit to determine how individual election officials in each county/state process and address problems with "motor voter" implementation based on his personal experience with being placed on the "inactive" voter roll despite registering his relocations promptly with the department of motor vehicles.

- ***Whether the absence of 'early voting' opportunities effectively disenfranchises some, including the poor.*** One SAC member noted the possible impact of the absence of early voting opportunities on the poor because of lack of transportation/ability to take time off work on election day. This member cited an effective program in Nevada to maximize voter turnout by providing numerous early voting locations and requiring employers to permit people to take up to three hours off to vote.

- ***The possibility that the use of paper ballots affords greater voting rights protections to minority communities than electronic ballots or voting machines.*** One SAC member expressed his opinion that some voting machines have been proven to be hackable/unreliable while others are much more tamperproof. He stressed that when the machines break down or do not tabulate votes correctly, a hand recount of the hard copy ballots is transparent and unequivocal. A member of the Ohio SAC echoed this belief, arguing that paper ballots obviously comprised a "paper trail" that is more difficult to obscure and erase than the electronic records of the current crop of voting machines.

- ***Disenfranchisement of ex-felons.*** A member of the Kentucky SAC stated that, in her state, the right to vote is denied to nearly 129,000 adults who had been in trouble with the law. According to her, Kentucky is one of only two states that permanently disenfranchises all persons with felony convictions even after completion of the full sentence. Also, as she writes, Kentucky has the sixth highest rate of disenfranchisement in the nation, and the highest African-American disenfranchisement rate in the country with nearly one in four African-Americans ineligible to vote.

Administration of Justice

- ***Employment restrictions placed on those convicted of misdemeanors and felonies.*** A member of the Illinois SAC recounted how such restrictions severely limit the ability of those convicted of misdemeanors and felons in her state to re-enter the workforce and make a meaningful contribution to society. She also credits returning to the workforce with limiting recidivism.

- ***The civil rights of children incarcerated in juvenile detention facilities.*** A member of the Illinois SAC related how the juvenile justice system in Illinois has been the subject of many reform efforts, alleging that some children are not receiving the assistance, treatment, and rehabilitation needed to become productive citizens. She cited a lawsuit filed by the ACLU in Illinois to require one juvenile detention center to provide safe and clean living conditions for the children under their care, and mentions that she believes the center is not complying with the settlement reached in the case.

Miscellaneous

- **The constraints placed by insufficient funding on state and federal agencies charged with enforcing equal employment opportunities.** A member of the Illinois SAC attributes a backlog in investigations at the Illinois Department of Human Rights and the state Equal Employment Opportunity Commission to insufficient funding for these agencies. According to her, insufficient funding prohibits these agencies from proactive enforcement activities and discourages potential complainants from pursuing discrimination claims.

- **Discrimination against poor and homeless individuals as a result of urban re-gentrification.** A Utah SAC member believed that efforts to push homeless people out of the way and scapegoat them for social ills never seems to go out of style, especially in the face of urban re-gentrification.

Important Civil Rights Issues: A Nationwide Perspective

The Office of the Staff Director tabulated the rankings of all SAC members regardless of state to identify the top civil rights issues and challenges nationwide.

Race/Color/National Origin
1. The racial/ethnic achievement gap in elementary and secondary education in public schools and its possible causes (e.g., family structure, culture, underfunded schools)
2. Racial disparities in health care access and outcomes, including inadequate health care, lack of health care access for lower income people, and denial of health care without proof of citizenship
3. The impact of minority neighborhoods plagued by crime, drugs and violence on access to education, and possible solutions to this problem (e.g., job training, assiduous policing, family structure)
4. Disparities in school expulsions and discipline of minority students in public schools
5. Disparate impact/treatment of racially identifiable populations in the contexts of law enforcement (racial profiling), sentencing, and incarceration (e.g., prison conditions, use of rehabilitative ex-offender programs)

Gender
1. Ensuring educational and extracurricular involvement of all students regardless of gender
2. Wage disparities between men and women
3. Lack of adequate legal protection for abused women and children
4. Lack of public contracting opportunities afforded to minority and women-owned businesses
5. Reverse gender discrimination in higher education student admissions and faculty hiring

Disability
1. Discrimination against people with mental health issues
2. The rights of the disabled to live independently free from nursing homes
3. State closure of institutional living for the developmentally disabled to provide available funding to community-based living for the same
4. Issues of physical access and accommodation for disabled individuals, including requests of the disabled and some non-disabled for unreasonable adjustments and special accommodations from employers and educational institutions
5. Employment discrimination against employees with mental impairments

Religion
1. Enforcement of separation of church and state in public schools, including efforts to ensure that religious instruction is not incorporated into public school curricula
2. Increase in religious discrimination, including against religious minorities and non-religious citizenry
3. The impact on civil rights of religious employers, health care providers and other individuals as a result of governmental mandates that contravene widely-subscribed religious beliefs (e.g., coverage of contraceptives in employer health care plans, provision of controversial medical care, recognition of same-sex marriage)

4. Religion-motivated hate crimes
5. Conflict between assertion of some civil rights and the rights of free exercise, freedom of speech, and freedom of assembly, e.g., possible increase in religious discrimination as a result of laws prohibiting discrimination on the basis of sexual orientation

Administration of Justice
1. Bias against racial/ethnic minorities in the administration of justice
2. Employment restrictions placed on those convicted of misdemeanors and felonies
3. Reparation civil rights regarding proven wrongful imprisonment

Voting Rights
1. The possibility that the use of paper ballots afford greater voting rights protections to minority communities than electronic ballots or voting machines
2. Voter rights regarding access, intimidation, and suppression of voting in minority residential areas
3. Whether the absence of "early voting" opportunities effectively disenfranchises some, including the poor
4. Disenfranchisement of ex-felons
5. Implementation and effectiveness of "motor voter" legislation

Miscellaneous
1. Marriage and equal rights for members of gay, lesbian, bisexual, and transgender community, and the Commission's position on these issues
2. Privacy rights regarding personal data held by public institutions, communication via e-mail, phone, Internet, and the federal government's access to this data in the context of national security
3. The constraints placed by insufficient funding on state and federal agencies charged with enforcing equal employment opportunities
4. Lack of affordable housing for minorities, women and disabled
5. Predatory lending

Important Civil Rights Issues: The Perspective from the States

ALABAMA

One member of the Alabama SAC submitted rankings:

Race/Color/National Origin
1. Impediments to African-American vendors receiving contracts from city, county, and state

ARKANSAS

Although no member of the Arkansas SAC submitted rankings, its members had identified the following as important civil rights issues:

- Closer examination of enforcement of Title VI of the Civil Rights Act of 1964 by the Office for Civil Rights, U.S. Department of Education in the region
- Prison conditions as they affect a racially identifiable population
- Hostile atmosphere directed at Hispanic residents stemming from suspected immigrant status
- Discrimination by federally funded Planned Parenthood by placing more offices in minority areas
- Illegal immigration issues, including proposition 187 and patrolling for criminal activity or waiting until it occurs
- Lack of law enforcement in combating drug use (meth, crack, and cocaine)
- The need for mechanisms to enable the federal government to report/relate/cooperate with state officials/offices in joint initiatives to assure the enforcement of civil rights laws and to educate the public about those laws

CALIFORNIA

Although no member of the California SAC submitted rankings, its members had identified the following as important civil rights issues:

- School choice and the racial/ethnic achievement gap in elementary and secondary education in public schools
- Racial and ethnic preferences in admissions in federally-funded colleges and universities
- Lack of enforcement of minority business enterprises (MBE) and women business enterprises (WBE) guidance in state and federal contracting
- Discrimination against Native Americans
- Discrimination against undocumented immigrant workers in education and employment
- Possible state underfunding of public schools and the impact on African-American and Hispanic students and families

- Increase in hate crimes against Arab-Americans and other immigrant groups after September 11, 2001
- Low graduation rates and educational disparities of minority students, as well as flawed data on dropout rates for these groups
- Disparities in school expulsions and discipline of minority students in public schools
- Re-segregation of American high schools in the 21st century, especially of Latino and African-American students
- Current state of migrant students and equal access to educational opportunities in the United States
- Civil rights of illegal immigrants who are employed and paying taxes
- Racial discrimination in employee recruitment, retention, and promotion
- Minority access to quality education
- Enforcement of/compliance with state civil rights initiatives that prohibit discrimination or preferential treatment on the basis of race in education, employment, or public contracting
- Requests of the disabled and some non-disabled for unreasonable adjustments and special accommodations from employers and educational institutions
- A clearer definition of separation of church and state in the context of religious and other student organizations facing in-school discrimination
- Reparation civil rights regarding proven wrongful imprisonment
- Inmates' right to quality health care
- Voter rights regarding access and suppression of voting
- Implementation and effectiveness of "motor voter" legislation
- Whether the absence of "early voting" opportunities effectively disenfranchises some, including the poor
- The reliability of voting machines
- Marriage and equal rights for members of the gay, lesbian, bisexual, and transgender community, and the position of the U.S. Commission on Civil Rights on these issues
- Preparation of foster and group home living children for the transition to independent living
- Privacy rights regarding personal data held by public institutions
- Privacy rights regarding communication via e-mail, phone, Internet
- Patients' right to know medical doctor's training, legal, and disciplinary history
- Racial discrimination in the judicial system, including parity in punishments

CONNECTICUT

Two members of the Connecticut SAC submitted rankings:

Religion
1. Conflict between assertion of some civil rights and the rights of free exercise, freedom of speech, and freedom of assembly, e.g., possible increase in religious discrimination as a result of laws prohibiting discrimination on the basis of sexual orientation
2. The impact on civil rights of religious employers, health care providers and other individuals as a result of governmental mandates that contravene widely-subscribed religious beliefs

(e.g., coverage of contraceptives in employer health care plans; provision of controversial medical care; recognition of same-sex marriage)
3. Religion-motivated hate crimes
4. Increase in religious discrimination, including against religious minorities and non-religious citizenry
5. A clearer definition of separation of church and state in the context of religious and other student organizations facing in-school discrimination

Race/Color/National Origin
1. Reverse racial discrimination in higher education student admissions and faculty hiring
2. Discrimination by federally funded Planned Parenthood by placing more offices in minority areas
3. The impact of minority neighborhoods plagued by crime, drugs and violence on access to education, and possible solutions to this problem (e.g., job training, assiduous policing, family structure)/ Enforcement of/compliance with state civil rights initiatives that prohibit discrimination or preferential treatment on the basis of race in education, employment, or public contracting
4. Racial and ethnic preferences in admissions in colleges and universities and their impact on intended beneficiaries/General ongoing problems with racial intolerance (tie)
5. The use of employment discrimination law concepts such as hostile environment as a justification for restrictions on freedom of expression in higher education

Prior to submitting rankings, members of the Connecticut SAC also identified the following as important civil rights issues:

*   Increase in religious discrimination in public education as a result of secularized curricula, religious expression by students, and religious immigrants
*   The extent to which religious organizations can hire based on religion when they receive government funding
*   Privacy concerns in the context of the federal government's access to personal information

FLORIDA

Two members of the Florida SAC submitted rankings:

Race/Color/National Origin
1. The racial/ethnic achievement gap in elementary and secondary education in public schools and its possible causes (e.g., family structure, culture, underfunded schools)
2. Enforcement of/compliance with state civil rights initiatives that prohibit discrimination or preferential treatment on the basis of race in education, employment, or public contracting
3. Reverse racial discrimination in higher education student admissions and faculty hiring
4. Enforcement of minority business enterprises (MBE) and women business enterprises (WBE) guidance in state and federal contracting, including race- and gender-based hiring goals, and the lack of opportunities for public contracting for these enterprises

5. Racial discrimination in employee recruitment, retention, and promotion/Reverse racial discrimination in federal agencies (tie)

Gender
1. Reverse gender discrimination in higher education student admissions and faculty hiring
2. Wage disparities between men and women
3. Lack of public contracting opportunities afforded to minority and women-owned businesses
4. Lack of adequate legal protection for abused women and children
5. Ensuring educational and extracurricular involvement of all students regardless of gender

Religion
1. The impact on civil rights of religious employers, health care providers and other individuals as a result of governmental mandates that contravene widely-subscribed religious beliefs (e.g., coverage of contraceptives in employer health care plans, provision of controversial medical care, recognition of same-sex marriage)
2. The extent to which religious organizations can hire based on religion when they receive government funding
3. Conflict between assertion of some civil rights and the rights of free exercise, freedom of speech, and freedom of assembly, e.g., possible increase in religious discrimination as a result of laws prohibiting discrimination on the basis of sexual orientation
4. Increase in religious discrimination in public education as a result of secularized curricula, religious expression by students, and religious immigrants
5. Increase in religious discrimination, including against religious minorities and non-religious citizenry

Disability
1. Discrimination against people with mental health issues
2. State closure of institutional living for the developmentally disabled to provide available funding to community-based living for the same
3. The rights of the disabled to live independently free from nursing homes
4. Employment discrimination against employees with mental impairments
5. Issues of physical access and accommodation for disabled individuals, including requests of the disabled and some non-disabled for unreasonable adjustments and special accommodations from employers and educational institutions

Voting Rights
1. Voter rights regarding access, intimidation, and suppression of voting in minority residential areas
2. Whether the absence of "early voting" opportunities effectively disenfranchises some, including the poor
3. The possibility that the use of paper ballots afford greater voting rights protections to minority communities than electronic ballots or voting machines
4. Disenfranchisement of ex-felons
5. Implementation and effectiveness of "motor voter" legislation

Administration of Justice
1. Bias against racial/ethnic minorities in the administration of justice
2. Reparation civil rights regarding proven wrongful imprisonment
3. Employment restrictions placed on those convicted of misdemeanors and felonies

Miscellaneous
1. The need for mechanisms to enable the federal government to report/relate/cooperate with state officials/offices in joint initiatives to assure the enforcement of civil rights laws and to educate the public about those laws
2. Privacy rights regarding personal data held by public institutions, communication via e-mail, phone, internet, and the federal government's access to this data in the context of national security
3. Lack of leadership and will to take action regarding anti-enforcement tools currently available and consideration of possible amendments to the Civil Rights Act of 1964 to make this possible/Marriage and equal rights for members of gay, lesbian, bisexual, and transgender community, and the Commission's position on these issues (tie)
4. Speedy, efficient and effective resolution of civil rights complaints
5. The role of discrimination in perpetuating disparities from generation to generation

GEORGIA

One member of the Georgia SAC submitted rankings:

Race/Color/National Origin
1. Possible racial resegregation of public secondary schools
2. Disparities in school expulsions and discipline of minority students in public schools
3. Disparate impact/treatment of racially identifiable populations in the contexts of law enforcement (racial profiling), sentencing, and incarceration (e.g., prison conditions, use of rehabilitative ex-offender programs)
4. Racial disparities in health care access and outcomes, including inadequate health care, lack of health care access for lower income people, and denial of health care without proof of citizenship

Gender
1. Ensuring educational and extracurricular involvement of all students regardless of gender

Disability
1. Discrimination against people with mental health issues

Religion
1. Increase in religious discrimination, including against religious minorities and non-religious citizenry

HAWAII

Two members of the Hawaii SAC submitted rankings:

Race/Color/National Origin
1. Discrimination against non-native Hawaiians in the provision of governmental services
2. Possible extension of tribal recognition and quasi-sovereignty to Native Hawaiians
3. The Office of Hawaiian Affairs' acceptance of certain state lands and cash in settlement of Native Hawaiian claims to reparations for the transfer of certain lands from the Hawaiian monarchy to the Republic of Hawaii and subsequently to the State of Hawaii

Prior to submitting rankings, another member of the Hawaii SAC had identified racial disparities in the criminal justice system as an important civil rights issue.

ILLINOIS

Two members of the Illinois SAC submitted rankings:

Race/Color/National Origin
1. State efforts to curtail illegal immigration, including initiatives to prohibit illegal immigrants' access to non-emergency health care, primary and secondary education, and other benefits, and whether these laws encroach on the federal government's role in immigration
2. Closer examination of enforcement of Title VI of the Civil Rights Act of 1964 (prohibition against racial discrimination in providing access to equal educational opportunities) by the Office for Civil Rights, U.S. Department of Education
3. The lack of comprehensive immigration law combining border security with respect for the dignity of the person and its contribution to the alienation of immigrants from participating in mainstream society
4. The civil rights of illegal immigrants who are employed and paying taxes/Disparate impact/treatment of racially identifiable populations in the contexts of law enforcement (racial profiling), sentencing, and incarceration (e.g., prison conditions, use of rehabilitative ex-offender programs) (tie)
5. Current state of migrant students and equal access to educational opportunities in the United States

Disability
1. State closure of institutional living for the developmentally disabled to provide available funding to community-based living for the same

Religion
1. Conflict between assertion of some civil rights and the rights of free exercise, freedom of speech, and freedom of assembly, e.g., possible increase in religious discrimination as a result of laws prohibiting discrimination on the basis of sexual orientation

Administration of Justice
1. Employment restrictions placed on those convicted of misdemeanors and felonies

Miscellaneous
1. Lack of leadership and will to take action regarding anti-enforcement tools currently available and consideration of possible amendments to the Civil Rights Act of 1964 to make this possible
2. The constraints placed by insufficient funding on state and federal agencies charged with enforcing equal employment opportunities

Prior to submitting rankings, members of the Illinois SAC also identified the following as important civil rights issues:

- Possible state underfunding of public schools and the impact on African-American and Hispanic students and families
- Race and national origin-motivated hate crimes
- Racial disparities in access to health care, education, housing and wealth
- Racial disparities in income and their relationship to racial disparities in housing, health care, education and employment
- The use rehabilitative ex-offender programs to reduce recidivism and the related racial inequities in the criminal justice system
- Racial disparities in high school graduation and retention rates for Latinos and African-Americans as well as racial disparities in college and graduation rates for Latinos and African-Americans
- Racial and gender disparities in the professorate regarding representation at the various levels of full professor, associate, and assistant
- Lack of adequate legal protection for abused women and children
- Employment discrimination against employees with mental impairments
- Religious discrimination in prisons
- Religion-motivated hate crimes
- The civil rights of children incarcerated in juvenile detention facilities
- Hate crime reporting and statistics regarding patterns in terms of foci (race, sexual orientation, religion, and immigration status)

INDIANA

Two members of the Indiana SAC submitted rankings:

Race/Color/National Origin
1. Racial disparities in health care, education, housing, wealth, and incarceration, and their relationship to each other and to possible causes, such as family structure and inherited intelligence potential that differs by individual/Enforcement of/compliance with state civil

rights initiatives that prohibit discrimination or preferential treatment on the basis of race in education, employment, or public contracting (tie)
2. Closer examination of enforcement of Title VI of the Civil Rights Act of 1964 (prohibition against racial discrimination in providing access to equal educational opportunities) by the Office for Civil Rights, U.S. Department of Education
3. Disparities in school expulsions and discipline of minority students in public schools
4. The racial/ethnic achievement gap in elementary and secondary education in public schools and its possible causes (e.g., family structure, culture, underfunded schools)
5. Racial and ethnic preferences in admissions in colleges and universities and their impact on intended beneficiaries

Gender
1. Wage disparities between men and women
2. Lack of public contracting opportunities afforded to minority and women-owned businesses
3. Reverse gender discrimination in higher education student admissions and faculty hiring
4. Ensuring educational and extracurricular involvement of all students regardless of gender
5. Lack of adequate legal protection for abused women and children

Religion
1. Enforcement of separation of church and state in public schools, including efforts to ensure that religious instruction is not incorporated into public school curricula
2. The impact on civil rights of religious employers, health care providers and other individuals as a result of governmental mandates that contravene widely-subscribed religious beliefs (e.g., coverage of contraceptives in employer health care plans, provision of controversial medical care, recognition of same-sex marriage)
3. Religion-motivated hate crimes
4. Religious discrimination in prisons
5. Religious discrimination in the context of national security

Disability
1. Issues of physical access and accommodation for disabled individuals, including requests of the disabled and some non-disabled for unreasonable adjustments and special accommodations from employers and educational institutions
2. Discrimination against people with mental health issues
3. Employment discrimination against employees with mental impairments
4. State closure of institutional living for the developmentally disabled to provide available funding to community-based living for the same
5. The rights of the disabled to live independently free from nursing homes

Voting Rights
1. The possibility that the use of paper ballots afford greater voting rights protections to minority communities than electronic ballots or voting machines
2. Disenfranchisement of ex-felons
3. Whether the absence of "early voting" opportunities effectively disenfranchises some, including the poor

4. Voter rights regarding access, intimidation, and suppression of voting in minority residential areas
5. Implementation and effectiveness of "motor voter" legislation

Miscellaneous
1. Marriage and equal rights for members of the gay, lesbian, bisexual, and transgender community, and the Commission's position on these issues
2. Lack of leadership and will to take action regarding anti-enforcement tools currently available and consideration of possible amendments to the Civil Rights Act of 1964 to make this possible
3. Privacy rights regarding personal data held by public institutions, communication via e-mail, phone, Internet, and the federal government's access to this data in the context of national security
4. Hate crime reporting and statistics regarding patterns in terms of foci (race, sexual orientation, religion, and immigration status), and the possible need for amended hate crimes legislation
5. Predatory lending

Administration of Justice
1. Employment restrictions placed on those convicted of misdemeanors and felonies
2. Bias against racial/ethnic minorities in the administration of justice
3. Reparation civil rights regarding proven wrongful imprisonment

Prior to submitting rankings, members of the Indiana SAC identified the following as important civil rights issues:

*   Comprehensive look at enforcement of the Culturally and Linguistically Appropriate Standards (CLAS) issued by the Department of Health and Human Services regarding the health needs of persons who, because of racial, ethnic, or linguistic reasons, may experience unequal access to health services
*   Lack of enforcement of minority business enterprises (MBE) and women business enterprises (WBE) guidance in state and federal contracting
*   Equity issues in education, employment, administration of justice, housing, and health care
*   Lack of choice for Medicaid recipients in managed care to obtain access to preventive health care support when the managed care organization is not providing adequate services, especially when there exists lock-in participation rules

KENTUCKY

Although no member of the Kentucky SAC had submitted rankings, its members had identified the following as important civil rights issues:

*   Provision of fair housing education and outreach programs to refugee communities across Kentucky

- The state's biannual report on women and minority employment in state agencies
- Ensuring educational and extracurricular involvement of all students regardless of race, gender or national origin
- Gender-based hiring goals of state agencies
- Disenfranchisement of ex-felons

MICHIGAN

Prior to submitting rankings, members of the Michigan SAC identified the following as important civil rights issues:

- Enforcement of/compliance with state civil rights initiatives that prohibit discrimination or preferential treatment on the basis race in education, employment, or public contracting
- Reverse discrimination in federal agencies
- Relationship between educational disparities and disparities in health, wealth, housing, incarceration rates, and the relationship of all these to family structure and inherited intelligence potential that differs by individual
- Equity

MISSISSIPPI

One member of the Mississippi SAC submitted rankings:

Race/Color/National Origin
1. Disparate impact/treatment of racially identifiable populations in the contexts of law enforcement (racial profiling), sentencing, and incarceration (e.g., prison conditions, use of rehabilitative ex-offender programs)
2. Racial discrimination in employee recruitment, retention, and promotion
3. Racial disparities in health care, education, housing, wealth, and incarceration, and their relationship to each other and to possible causes, such as family structure and inherited intelligence potential differs by individual
4. Disparities in school expulsions and discipline of minority students in public schools
5. Racial disparities in health care access and outcomes, including inadequate health care, lack of health care access for lower income people, and denial of health care without proof of citizenship

Disability
1. Employment discrimination against employees with mental impairments

Administration of Justice
1. Bias against racial/ethnic minorities in the administration of justice

Miscellaneous

1. Hate crime reporting and statistics regarding patterns in terms of foci (race, sexual orientation, religion, and immigration status), and the possible need for amended hate crimes legislation
2. The civil rights of children incarcerated in juvenile detention facilities

Prior to submitting rankings, members of the Mississippi SAC had identified predatory lending as an important civil rights issue.

NORTH CAROLINA

One member of the North Carolina SAC submitted rankings:

Race/Color/National Origin
1. The disparate impact of the housing crisis on African-Americans and Hispanics
2. Possible racial resegregation of public secondary schools
3. Disparities in school expulsions and discipline of minority students in public schools
4. The racial/ethnic achievement gap in elementary and secondary education in public schools and its possible causes
5. Racial disparities in health care access and outcomes, including inadequate health care, lack of health care access for lower income people, and denial of health care without proof of citizenship

Prior to submitting rankings, members of the North Carolina SAC identified the following as important civil rights issues:

- Inequalities in the prison population and in the criminal justice system
- Substandard housing
- Substandard economic development
- Inadequate health care and lack of availability of health care facilities in many areas

NEW JERSEY

Two members of the New Jersey SAC submitted rankings:

Miscellaneous
1. Evidence that students are forced to attend schools in which they reasonably fear for their physical safety/lives
2. Allegations that school administrators are lying/misreporting the number and severity of violent incidents to deprive students of their federal rights under No Child Left Behind

Disability
1. State closure of institutional living for the developmentally disabled to provide available funding to community based living for the same

2. Right of people with disabilities to live independently free from nursing homes
3. Legitimize specific concerns of people of color with disabilities
4. Resources to document dual discrimination and access for people of color with disabilities

OHIO

Four members of the Ohio SAC submitted rankings:

Race/Color/National Origin
1. Racial disparities in health care access and outcomes, including inadequate health care, lack of health care access for lower income people, and denial of health care without proof of citizenship
2. The disparate impact of the housing crisis on African-Americans and Hispanics
3. The racial/ethnic achievement gap in elementary and secondary education in public schools and its possible causes (e.g., family structure, culture, underfunded schools)
4. Disparate impact/treatment of racially identifiable populations in the contexts of law enforcement (racial profiling), sentencing, and incarceration (e.g., prison conditions, use of rehabilitative ex-offender programs) , and the impact of drug decriminalization on these populations
5. Disparities in school expulsion and discipline of minority students in public schools

Gender
1. Lack of adequate legal protection for abused women and children
2. Ensuring educational and extracurricular involvement of all students regardless of gender
3. Wage disparities between men and women
4. Reverse gender discrimination in higher education student admissions and faculty hiring

Disability
1. Issues of physical access and accommodation for disabled individuals, including requests of the disabled and some non-disabled for unreasonable adjustments and special accommodations from employers and educational institutions
2. Discrimination (including employment) against people with mental health issues
3. The rights of the disabled to live independently free from nursing homes

Religion
1. Increase in religious discrimination, including against religious minorities and non-religious citizenry
2. Enforcement of separation of church and state in public schools, including efforts to ensure that religious instruction is not incorporated into public school curricula
3. Religious discrimination in the context of national security
4. Conflict between assertion of some civil rights and the rights of free exercise, freedom of speech, and freedom of assembly, e.g., possible increase in religious discrimination as a result of laws prohibiting discrimination on the basis of sexual orientation

5. A clearer definition of separation of church and state in the context of religious and other student organizations facing in-school discrimination

Administration of Justice
1. Employment restrictions placed on those convicted of misdemeanors and felonies
2. Bias against racial/ethnic minorities in the administration of justice
3. Reparation civil rights regarding proven wrongful imprisonment

Voting Rights
1. Voter rights regarding access, intimidation, and suppression of voting in minority residential areas
2. The possibility that the use of paper ballots afford greater voting rights protections to minority communities than electronic ballots or voting machines
3. Whether the absence of "early voting" opportunities effectively disenfranchises some, including the poor
4. Disenfranchisement of ex-felons
5. Implementation and effectiveness of "motor voter" legislation

Miscellaneous
1. Privacy rights regarding personal data held by public institutions, communication via e-mail, phone, Internet, and the federal government's access to this data in the context of national security
2. Marriage and equal rights for members of the gay, lesbian, bisexual, and transgender community, and the Commission's position on these issues
3. Predatory lending
4. Lack of affordable housing for minorities, women and disabled
5. The constraints placed by insufficient funding on state and federal agencies charged with enforcing equal employment opportunities/The role of discrimination in perpetuating disparities from generation to generation (tie)

Prior to submitting rankings, members of the Ohio SAC had also identified reverse racial discrimination in higher education student admissions and faculty hiring as an important civil rights issue.

OKLAHOMA

Three members of the Oklahoma SAC submitted rankings.

Race/Color/National Origin
1. The racial/ethnic achievement gap in elementary and secondary education in public schools and its possible causes (e.g., family structure, culture, underfunded schools)
2. Discrimination against Hispanics (or persons perceived to be Hispanic), including hate crimes based on Hispanic origin/ School choice aimed at ensuring that every child, regardless

of race or socioeconomic background, has an opportunity to attend the safest and best schools, whether those schools are public or private (tie)

3. Discrimination by federally funded Planned Parenthood by placing more offices in minority areas/ Enforcement of minority business enterprises (MBE) and women business enterprises (WBE) guidance in state and federal contracting, including race- and gender-based hiring goals, and the lack of opportunities for public contracting for these enterprises (tie)

4. Racial disparities in health care, education, housing, wealth, and incarceration, and their relationship to each other and to possible causes, such as family structure and inherited intelligence potential that differs by individual / State efforts to curtail illegal immigration, including initiatives to prohibit illegal immigrants' access to non-emergency health care, primary and secondary education, and other benefits, and whether these laws encroach on the federal government's role in immigration (tie)

5. Discrimination against persons perceived to be Muslim and/or of Middle Eastern ancestry/The civil rights of illegal immigrants who are employed and paying taxes (tie)

Gender
1. Wage disparities between men and women
2. Lack of public contracting opportunities afforded to minority and women-owned businesses
3. Lack of adequate legal protection for abused women and children

Religion
1. The impact on civil rights of religious employers, health care providers and other individuals as a result of governmental mandates that contravene widely-subscribed religious beliefs (e.g., coverage of contraceptives in employer health care plans, provision of controversial medical care, recognition of same-sex marriage)

Miscellaneous
1. Discrimination/hate crimes targeting the gay/lesbian/bisexual/transgendered community

PENNSYLVANIA

One member of the Pennsylvania SAC submitted rankings:

Race/Color/National Origin
1. Disparate impact/treatment of racially identifiable populations in the contexts of law enforcement (racial profiling), sentencing, and incarceration (e.g., prison conditions, use of rehabilitative ex-offender programs) , and the impact of drug decriminalization on these populations

Prior to submitting rankings, members of the Pennsylvania SAC identified the following as important civil rights issues:

*   Prevalence of multiple languages and prejudice
*   Government-inspired xenophobia in the face of continued immigration

- Lack of public contracting opportunities afforded to minority and women-owned businesses
- Tensions between privacy rights and the reasonable need for security
- Equity in the arts
- Concerns about individuals' equal access to the courts regardless of income, exacerbated by the costs of a legal education and establishing a law practice
- Speedy, efficient and effective resolution of civil rights complaints
- The role of discrimination in perpetuating disparities from generation to generation
- Affordability of education for all in the United States

RHODE ISLAND

Two members of the Rhode Island SAC submitted rankings:

Race/Color/National Origin:
1. The impact of minority neighborhoods plagued by crime, drugs and violence on access to education, and possible solutions to this problem (e.g., job training, assiduous policing, family structure)
2. The racial/ethnic achievement gap in elementary and secondary education in public schools and its possible causes (e.g., family structure, culture, underfunded schools)
3. Racial disparities in health care, education, housing, wealth, and incarceration, and their relationship to each other and to possible causes, such as family structure and inherited intelligence potential that differs by individual/race and national origin-motivated hate crimes, including hate crimes against Arab-Americans and other immigrant groups after September 11, 2001 (tie)
4. The disparate impact of the housing crisis on African-Americans and Hispanics
5. Disparate impact/treatment of racially identifiable populations in the contexts of law enforcement (racial profiling), sentencing, and incarceration (e.g., prison conditions, use of rehabilitative ex-offender programs)

Gender
1. Lack of adequate legal protection for abused women and children
2. Ensuring educational and extracurricular involvement of all students regardless of gender

Disability
1. Issues of physical access and accommodation for disabled individuals, including requests of the disabled and some non-disabled for unreasonable adjustments and special accommodations from employers and educational institutions
2. Discrimination against people with mental health issues

Religion
1. Enforcement of separation of church and state in public schools, including efforts to ensure that religious instruction is not incorporated into public school curricula
2. Religion-motivated hate crimes

Administration of Justice
1. Bias against racial/ethnic minorities in the administration of justice
2. Reparation civil rights regarding proven wrongful imprisonment

Voting Rights
1. Whether the absence of "early voting" opportunities effectively disenfranchises some, including the poor/Implementation and effectiveness of "motor voter" legislation (tie)

Miscellaneous
1. Lack of affordable housing for minorities, women and disabled
2. Affordability of education for all in the United States

SOUTH CAROLINA

One member of the South Carolina SAC submitted rankings:

Race/Color/National Origin
1. The racial/ethnic achievement gap in elementary and secondary education in public schools and its possible causes (e.g., family structure, culture, underfunded schools)
2. Employment of racial/ethnic minorities in state agencies (with special attention to senior and executive-level positions)
3. Possible racial resegregation of public secondary schools

Gender
1. Employment of women in state agencies (with special attention to senior and executive-level positions)

Miscellaneous
1. Predatory lending

Prior to submitting rankings, a member of the South Carolina SAC identified the provision of equal educational opportunities to disadvantaged students of color as an important civil rights issue.

TENNESSEE

One member of the Tennessee SAC submitted rankings, ranking the general issues of race/color/national origin, voting rights, disability, gender, and religion in descending order of importance.

TEXAS

Two members of the Texas SAC submitted rankings:

Race/Color/National Origin
1. The racial/ethnic achievement gap in elementary and secondary education in public schools and its possible causes (e.g., family structure, culture, underfunded schools)
2. Closer examination of enforcement of Title VI of the Civil Rights Act of 1964 (prohibition against racial discrimination in providing access to equal educational opportunities) by the Office for Civil Rights, U.S. Department of Education
3. Racial disparities in health care access and outcomes, including inadequate health care, lack of health care access for lower income people, and denial of health care without proof of citizenship/Enforcement of/compliance with state civil rights initiatives that prohibit discrimination or preferential treatment on the basis of race in education, employment, or public contracting (tie)
4. Possible racial resegregation of public secondary schools/State efforts to curtail immigration, including initiatives to prohibit illegal immigrants' access to non-emergency access to health care, primary and secondary education, and other benefits, and whether these laws encroach on the federal government's role in immigration (tie)
5. Disparities in school expulsions and discipline of minority students in public schools/ Employment of women and racial/ethnic minorities in state agencies (tie)

Gender
1. Wage disparities between men and women
2. Ensuring educational and extracurricular involvement of all students regardless of gender
3. Alleged lack of public contracting opportunities afforded to minority and women-owned businesses
4. Lack of adequate legal protection for abused women and children
5. Reverse gender discrimination in higher education student admissions and faculty hiring

Disability
1. State closure of institutional living for the developmentally disabled to provide available funding to community-based living for the same
2. The rights of the disabled to live independently free from nursing homes
3. Discrimination against people with mental health issues
4. Employment discrimination against employees with mental impairments
5. Issues of physical access and accommodation for disabled individuals, including requests of the disabled and some non-disabled for unreasonable adjustments and special accommodations from employers and educational institutions

Religion
1. Enforcement of separation of church and state in public schools, including efforts to ensure that religious instruction is not incorporated into public school curricula
2. Religion-motivated hate crimes
3. Increase in religious discrimination, including against religious minorities and non-religious citizenry
4. Religious discrimination in prisons

5. The extent to which religious organizations can hire based on religion when they receive government funding

Administration of Justice
1. Bias against racial/ethnic minorities in the administration of justice
2. Employment restrictions placed on those convicted of misdemeanors and felonies
3. Reparation civil rights regarding proven wrongful imprisonment

Voting Rights
1. Voter rights regarding access, intimidation, and suppression of voting in minority residential areas
2. The possibility that the use of paper ballots afford greater voting rights protections to minority communities than electronic ballots or voting machines
3. Disenfranchisement of ex-felons
4. Whether the absence of "early voting" opportunities effectively disenfranchises some, including the poor
5. Implementation and effectiveness of "motor voter" legislation

Miscellaneous
1. The need for mechanisms to enable the federal government to report/relate/cooperate with state officials/offices in joint initiatives to assure the enforcement of civil rights laws and to educate the public about those laws
2. The constraints placed by insufficient funding on state and federal agencies charged with enforcing equal employment opportunities/Marriage and equal rights for members of the gay, lesbian, bisexual, and transgender community, and the Commission's position on these issues (tie)
3. The civil rights of children incarcerated in juvenile detention facilities
4. Affordability of education for all in the United States
5. Lack of affordable housing for minorities, women and the disabled

Prior to submitting rankings, members of the Texas SAC identified the following as important civil rights issues:

*   The lack of comprehensive immigration (combining border security with respect for the dignity of the person) and its contribution to the alienation of immigrants from participating in mainstream society
*   Disparity in state funding of public school districts and the impact on African-American and Hispanic students and families
*   Disparate impact/treatment of racially identifiable populations in the contexts of law enforcement (racial profiling), sentencing, and incarceration (e.g., prison conditions, use of rehabilitative ex-offender programs)
*   Disparities in dropout rates among minorities in high school
*   Provision of fair housing education and outreach programs to refugee communities
*   Ensuring educational and extracurricular involvement of all students regardless of race or national origin

- Discrimination against undocumented immigrant workers in the areas of education and employment
- Wage disparities between whites and people of color of the same gender
- Racial/ethnic discrimination in the hiring and assignment of professional staff in public schools
- Discrimination against individuals of Hispanic origin based on race or presumed immigration status
- Gender-based hiring goals of state agencies
- Wage disparities between men and women
- General ongoing problems of religious intolerance
- Discrimination resulting from the religious motivated limitations on health care coverage
- Substandard housing
- The role of discrimination in perpetuating disparities from generation to generation
- Privacy rights regarding personal data held by public institutions, communication via e-mail, phone, Internet, and the federal government's access to this data in the context of national security

UTAH

Although no member of the Utah SAC submitted rankings, its members identified the following as important civil rights issues:

- Disparities in school expulsions and discipline of minority students in public schools
- Discrimination against individuals of Hispanic origin based on race or presumed immigration status
- Discrimination against Native Americans
- Racial discrimination in the context of national security
- Disparate impact/treatment of racially identifiable populations in the contexts of law enforcement (racial profiling), sentencing, and incarceration (e.g., prison conditions, use of rehabilitative ex-offender programs)
- Discrimination against undocumented immigrant workers in the areas of education and employment
- General ongoing problems with racial intolerance
- The racial/ethnic achievement gap in elementary and secondary education in public schools and its possible causes
- Foreign, non-resident students filling resident minority slots in state educational institutions
- Wage disparities between men and women
- The rights of the disabled to live independently free from nursing homes
- General ongoing problems of religious intolerance
- Religious discrimination in the context of national security
- Bias against minorities in the administration of justice
- Discrimination against poor and homeless individuals as a result of urban re-gentrification

- Employment discrimination in Utah, including a federal lawsuit alleging that the UALD (Utah Antidiscrimination and Labor Division) is itself engaged in discriminatory practices
- Possible racial disparate impact of employers' use of credit reports in hiring decisions
- The need for hate crimes legislation

VERMONT

Although no member of the Vermont SAC submitted rankings, its members identified civil rights issues arising from the state's transition from a racially homogenous to racially heterogeneous state population.

VIRGINIA

Two members of the Virginia SAC submitted rankings:

Race/Color/National Origin
1. The lack of comprehensive immigration law combining border security with respect for the dignity of the person and its contribution to the alienation of immigrants from participating in mainstream society
2. Enforcement of minority business enterprises (MBE) and women business enterprises (WBE) guidance in state and federal contracting, including race- and gender-based hiring goals, and the lack of opportunities for public contracting for these enterprises/ The impact of minority neighborhoods plagued by crime, drugs and violence on access to education, and possible solutions to this problem (e.g., job training, assiduous policing, family structure) (tie)
3. The racial/ethnic achievement gap in elementary and secondary education in public schools and its possible causes (e.g., family structure, culture, underfunded schools)/ Racial/ethnic discrimination in the hiring and assignment of professional staff in public schools (tie)
4. Racial disparities in health care, education, housing, wealth, and incarceration, and their relationship to each other and to possible causes, such as family structure and inherited intelligence potential that differs by individual/Wage disparities between whites and people of color of the same gender (tie)
5. Racial disparities in health care access and outcomes, including inadequate health care, lack of health care access for lower income people, and denial of health care without proof of citizenship/Reverse racial discrimination in higher education student admissions and faculty hiring (tie)

Gender
1. Reverse gender discrimination in higher education student admissions and faculty hiring

Religion
1. The impact on civil rights of religious employers, health care providers and other individuals as a result of governmental mandates that contravene widely-subscribed religious beliefs

(e.g., coverage of contraceptives in employer health care plans, provision of controversial medical care, recognition of same-sex marriage)
2. The extent to which religious organizations can hire based on religion when they receive government funding
3. Religious discrimination in the context of national security
4. Conflict between assertion of some civil rights and the rights of free exercise, freedom of speech, and freedom of assembly, e.g., possible increase in religious discrimination as a result of laws prohibiting discrimination on the basis of sexual orientation

Administration of Justice
1. Bias against racial/ethnic minorities in the administration of justice/Reparation civil rights regarding wrongful imprisonment (tie)

Miscellaneous
1. The constraints placed by insufficient funding on state and federal agencies charged with enforcing equal employment opportunities/Privacy rights regarding personal data held by public institutions, communication via e-mail, phone, Internet, and the federal government's access to this data in the context of national security (tie)
2. Speedy, efficient and effective resolution of civil rights complaints/Prison rape (tie)

WISCONSIN

One member of the Wisconsin SAC submitted rankings:

Race/Color/National Origin
1. Racial and ethnic preferences in admissions in colleges and universities and their impact on intended beneficiaries
2. Reverse racial discrimination in higher education student admissions and faculty hiring
3. Racial/ethnic discrimination in the hiring and assignment of professional staff in public schools
4. Racial discrimination in employee recruitment, retention, and promotion
5. The use of employment discrimination law concepts such as hostile environment as a justification for restrictions on freedom of expression in higher education

This member then ranked the general issues of voting rights, religion, disability, gender, administration of justice, and miscellaneous issues in descending order.

Prior to submitting rankings, members of the Wisconsin SAC also identified the following as important civil rights issues:

- Possible racial disparate impact of employers' use of credit reports in hiring decisions
- Disparate impact/treatment of racially identifiable populations in the contexts of law enforcement (racial profiling), sentencing, and incarceration (e.g., prison conditions, use of rehabilitative ex-offender programs)

- Racial disparities in health care access and outcomes, including inadequate health care, lack of health care access for lower income people, and denial of health care without proof of citizenship
- Institutional racism within various primary education systems, e.g., discrimination against African-Americans in Waukesha County
- The racial/ethnic achievement gap in elementary and secondary education in public schools and its possible causes (e.g., family structure, culture, underfunded schools)
- Discrimination against people with mental health issues

WYOMING

One member of the Wyoming SAC submitted rankings:

Race/Color/National Origin
1. Discrimination against Native Americans
2. The racial/ethnic achievement gap in elementary and secondary education in public schools and its possible causes (e.g., family structure, culture, underfunded schools)
3. Racial disparities in health care access and outcomes, including inadequate health care, lack of health care access for lower income people, and denial of health care without proof of citizenship
4. Reverse racial discrimination in federal agencies

Gender
1. Wage disparities between men and women

Religion
1. A clearer definition of separation of church and state in the context of religious and other student organizations facing in-school discrimination
2. Increase in religious discrimination in public education as a result of secularized curricula, religious expression by students, and religious immigrants

Miscellaneous
1. The role of discrimination in perpetuating disparities from generation to generation
2. Affordability of education for all in the United States
3. The need for mechanisms to enable the federal government to report/relate/cooperate with state officials/offices in joint initiatives to assure the enforcement of civil rights laws and to educate the public about those laws
4. The constraints placed by insufficient funding on state and federal agencies charged with enforcing equal employment opportunities
5. Privacy rights regarding personal data held by public institutions, communication via e-mail, phone, Internet, and the federal government's access to this data in the context of national security